discoveringFaith

THE GATHERING PLACE SERIES
A project guided by Daryl L. Smith

The Gathering Place: a series of books for people interested in exploring faith issues in a non-threatening setting. Each book uses questions, Bible selections, discussion, and group service as means for this exploration.

Don•Q•Dox: a resource-creation label of The Orlando Fellowship—
an incarnational, missional-ministry community.
  Don•Q—The fictional knight *Don Quixote* (Miguel de Cervantes, 1605), whose most famous adventure includes meeting the tavern prostitute Aldonza and calling her to become the beautiful Dulcinea.
  •Dox—Documents/tools/vehicles for discovery.

As the name implies, we are on a quest to discover life as it was meant to be and invite others to join that quest. We believe that God's image is planted deeply within each of us, but most times we cannot hear the call of the "impossible dream" without the company of others who can see in us things we don't see in ourselves.

discoveringFaith

8 Small Group Sessions PLUS Leader Resources

David M. Solano

RESOURCE *Publications* • Eugene, Oregon

DISCOVERING FAITH
8 Small Group Lesson PLUS Leader Resources

Copyright © 2013 David M. Solano. All rights reserved. Except for brief quotations in critical publications or reviews, no part of this book may be reproduced in any manner without prior written permission from the publisher. Write: Permissions, Wipf and Stock Publishers, 199 W. 8th Ave., Suite 3, Eugene, OR 97401.

Scripture quotations mared MSG are taken from *The Message*, copyright © 1993, 1994, 1995, 1996, 2000, 2001, 2002. Used by permission of NavPress Publishing Group. All rights reserved.

Resource Publications
An Imprint of Wipf and Stock Publishers
199 W. 8th Ave., Suite 3
Eugene, OR 97401
www.wipfandstock.com

ISBN 13: 978-1-62032-914-6

Manufactured in the U.S.A.

Interior Design: David M. Solano

Special thanks to Jonathan Blackburn for assisting in this project. Jonathan is an MACL graduate from Asbury Seminary—Kentucky, and is currently working on a PhD in intercultural studies.

CONTENTS

Session 1: Taking the Big Risk 1
(Matth w 14:22–33)

Session 2: Breaking Free from Religion... 6
(Matth w 11:20–30)

Session 3: All My Stuff... 10
Mark 10:17–30)

Session 4: Surviving Rejectio 14
(Mark 4:14–30)

Session 5: The Talk of the Town 18
(Mark 5:1–20)

Session 6: Searching for Wholeness 22
(Luke 8:43–48)

Session 7: Healing Those Strained Relationshi s...25
(Genesis 33:1–17)

Session 8: Thinking Great Ideas 29
(Philippians 4:4–9)

Celebrate the Group 33

Group Leader Notes 35

We Serve Together 45

Discovering Faith #1

TAKING THE BIG RISK

THE BIG IDEA
Life is filled with risks. Some are worth taking and some are not. The tough part is deciding which are which. In this Bible story, the disciples (Jesus-followers) had just come from watching Jesus perform a great miracle—feeding thousands of people with a couple of fish and some bread. Yet, most were not ready to believe that Jesus could care for them when the storm came. So, while the other disciples hovered in the boat, Peter took the risk and stepped out of the boat to go meet Jesus. Note the rewards and disappointments that Peter faced for taking the big risk.

OPEN:
1. What is your earliest memory of a traumatic experience in water?

    How did you respond to it?

    How did it change you?

READ AND APPLY :: Matthew 14:22-33 (MSG)

22-23 As soon as the meal was finished, he [Jesus] insisted that the disciples get in the boat and go on ahead to the other side while he dismissed the people. With the crowd dispersed, he climbed the mountain so he could be by himself and pray. He stayed there alone, late into the night.

24-26 Meanwhile, the boat was far out to sea when the wind came up against them and they were battered by the waves. At about four o'clock in the morning, Jesus came toward them walking on the water. They were scared out of their wits.

"A ghost!" they said, crying out in terror.
²⁷ But Jesus was quick to comfort them. "Courage, it's me. Don't be afraid."
²⁸ Peter, suddenly bold, said, "Master, if it's really you, call me to come to you on the water."
²⁹⁻³⁰ He said, "Come ahead." Jumping out of the boat, Peter walked on the water to Jesus. But when he looked down at the waves churning beneath his feet, he lost his nerve and started to sink. He cried, "Master, save me!"
³¹ Jesus didn't hesitate. He reached down and grabbed his hand. Then he said, "Faint-heart, what got into you?"
³²⁻³³ The two of them climbed into the boat, and the wind died down. The disciples in the boat, having watched the whole thing, worshiped Jesus, saying, "This is it! You are God's Son for sure!"

2. If you had been sitting with the disciples in the boat, waves splashing over the edge, what would have been your first instinct when Jesus came across the water?

   a. Let me out of here now!
   b. Cover me with something quick. I don't want him to see me.
   c. Hey, I want to try that cool trick, too.
   d. Sure hope he's here to stop these waves.
   e. Other _____

3. When Peter was bold enough to actually step over the side of the boat, what do you think the other disciples were saying to themselves?

   a. Wow! How's he doing that?
   b. Has Peter gone completely crazy?
   c. Peter is always stealing the spotlight! Why didn't Jesus call me instead!?
   d. Where's a camera when you need one!
   e. Other _____

4. If you had been a reporter hiding in the fishing nets in the boāom of the boat, who would you have most wanted to interview when you got to shore?

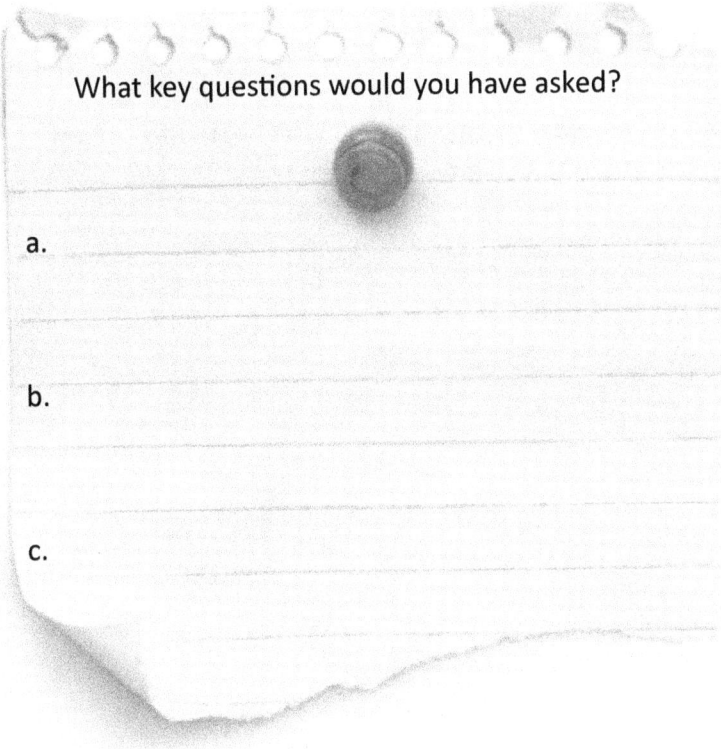

What key questions would you have asked?

a.

b.

c.

5. When it comes to Peter, what do you most identi y with?

   a. *"Master, if it's really you, call me to come to you on the water."* (Willing to trust, but waiting for a clear signal.)
   b. Peter jumping out of the boat. (I don't know if this is God or not…but oh, what the hay!)
   c. Peter looking down at the waves churning beneath his feet, losing nerve and beginning to sink. (The circumstances I find myself in always seem to shake my footing.
   d. *"Master, save me!"* (I need God for a bailout plan.)
   e. Other _____

THE ACCOUNTABLE COMMUNITY:

6. When you look at the enti e story, which part most relates to where you are living right now?

7. On the scale below (with 7 being the highest) CIRCLE how likely are you to take big risks:

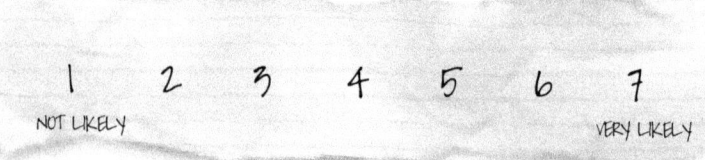

What are you willing to take the BIG RISK for?

   a. To gain financially or get more stuÃ.
   b. To help my family.
   c. To discover who Jesus really is.
   d. I don't really know right now.
   e. Other _____

8. What is the most risky part, when you think about Jesus?

   What questions would you like to have answered?

   a.

   b.

   c.

9. How might this group help you begin trusting (having faith in) Jesus with your life?

   How can we pray for you right now?

   > PRAY SILENTLY FOR THE PERSON ON YOUR LEFT,
   > THEN LET THE LEADER CLOSE OUT LOUD.

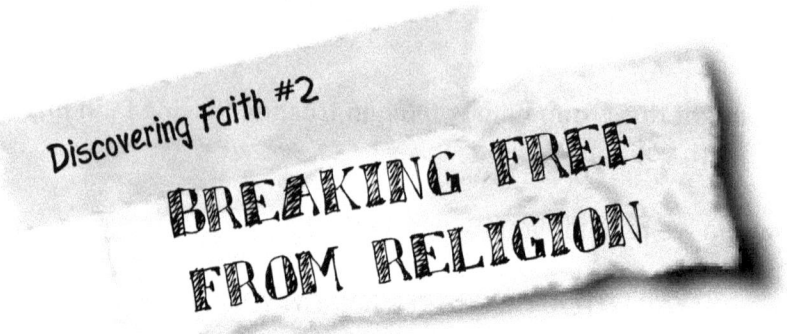

THE BIG IDEA:
Religion always seems to hang us up on discovering true faith. Even Jesus found that to be true. During his travels to several cities in his country, he performed many miracles of healing. Unfortunately, most of the people were so wrapped up in their religious stuff that they wouldn't believe in him or become his followers.

OPEN:
1. As a young teen in school, what was your most difficult subject? What made it particularly hard for you? How did you feel when you finally caught the new concepts? Or did you?

READ AND APPLY :: Matthew 11:20-30 (MSG)

[20] *Next Jesus let fly on the cities where he had worked the hardest but whose people had responded the least, shrugging their shoulders and going their own way.*
[21-24] *"Doom to you, Chorazin! Doom, Bethsaida! If Tyre and Sidon had seen half of the powerful miracles you have seen, they would have been on their knees in a minute. At Judgment Day they'll get off easy compared to you. And Capernaum! With all your peacock strutting, you are going to end up in the abyss. If the people of Sodom had had your chances, the city would still be around. At Judgment Day they'll get off easy compared to you."*
[25-26] *Abruptly Jesus broke into prayer: "Thank you, Father, Lord of heaven and earth. You've concealed your ways from sophisticates and know-it-alls, but spelled them out clearly to ordinary people. Yes, Father, that's the way you like to work."*

27 Jesus resumed talking to the people, but now tenderly. "The Father has given me all these things to do and say. This is a unique Father-Son operation, coming out of Father and Son intimacies and knowledge. No one knows the Son the way the Father does, nor the Father the way the Son does. But I'm not keeping it to myself; I'm ready to go over it line by line with anyone willing to listen.

28-30 "Are you tired? Worn out? Burned out on religion? Come to me. Get away with me and you'll recover your life. I'll show you how to take a real rest. Walk with me and work with me—watch how I do it. Learn the unforced rhythms of grace. I won't lay anything heavy or ill-fitting on you. Keep company with me and you'll learn to live freely and lightly."

2. If you had been in the crowd listening to Jesus teach, which group do you think you would have most identified with?

   a. The sophisti ated religious crowd.
   b. Those who were honestly searching for answers to who this Jesus was.
   c. The people who quickly jumped on board to follow Jesus.
   d. The folk just there to watch the "show."
   e. Other _____

3. Look again at verses 20–24, but this Āme make it personal. REPLACE one of the cities (Chorazin or Bethsaida) with the name of the city or neighborhood YOU live in.

   How do you think Jesus' words would make you feel?

   a. Terrifie
   b. "Um, yeah. I'm going to move...tomorrow."
   c. "Everyone in my city is going to go to heaven—this doesn't apply to me!"
   d. Other _____

4. What other words would you use to define the people that Jesus called "know-it-alls" and "ordinary people" (verse 25–26)?

   a. "Know-it-all" =

   b. "Ordinary people" =

5. What part of religion has burned you out, or worn you out as Jesus described? Why?

THE ACCOUNTABLE COMMUNITY:

6. As you look at your current faith journey, where do you see yourself as a "know-it-all" person—getting y on your own?

   Where do you see yourself as an "ordinary" person—open to exploring a relationship with God?

7. The "know-it-all" attitude an prevent us from discovering God's ways—or even beginning a faith relationship. Where do you need a special insight to help you become more "ordinary" in your attitud

8. If you could "live freely and lightly," as Jesus describes, how do you think your life would be different?

9. How can this group best support you in this journey this week?

10. How do you need the group to pray for you right now?

> LET THE LEADER CLOSE BY PRAYING OUT LOUD.

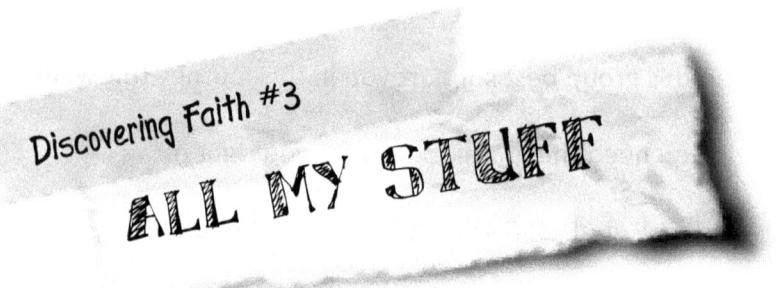

Discovering Faith #3
ALL MY STUFF

THE BIG IDEA:
In this Bible story a successful young man encounters Jesus to ask how one becomes a Jesus-follower. In the ensuing discussion, Jesus forces the man to face his real priorities in life. But Jesus doesn't stop there. He goes on to use that encounter as a teaching moment for his disciples—exposing the life-priority decisions all must make to truly follow Jesus.

OPEN:
1. You have inherited $100,000 to spend just for fun. How will you spend it?
   (Put a dollar amount by each item until you've spent the enti e $100,000. Once each person has completed their "spending," each will share their list with the group.)

   __ Great new _____ car
   __ New house in _____
   __ Vacation to _____
   __ Stocks/Bonds
   __ Donation to _____
   __ College fund for kids
   __ Toys for _____
   __ Help _____
   __ Other _____
   __ Other _____

READ AND APPLY :: Mark 10:17-31 (MSG)

¹⁷ As he went out into the street, a man came running up, greeted him with great reverence, and asked, "Good Teacher, what must I do to get eternal life?"

¹⁸⁻¹⁹ Jesus said, "Why are you calling me good? No one is good, only God. You know the commandments: Don't murder, don't commit adultery, don't steal, don't lie, don't cheat, honor your father and mother."

²⁰ He said, "Teacher, I have—from my youth—kept them all!"

²¹ Jesus looked him hard in the eye—and loved him! He said, "There's one thing left: Go sell whatever you own and give it to the poor. All your wealth will then be heavenly wealth. And come follow me."

²² The man's face clouded over. This was the last thing he expected to hear, and he walked off with a heavy heart. He was holding on tight to a lot of things, and not about to let go.

²³⁻²⁵ Looking at his disciples, Jesus said, "Do you have any idea how difficult it is for people who 'have it all' to enter God's kingdom?" The disciples couldn't believe what they were hearing, but Jesus kept on: "You can't imagine how difficult. I'd say it's easier for a camel to go through a needle's eye than for the rich to get into God's kingdom."

²⁶ That set the disciples back on their heels. "Then who has any chance at all?" they asked.

²⁷ Jesus was blunt: "No chance at all if you think you can pull it off by yourself. Every chance in the world if you let God do it."

²⁸ Peter tried another angle: "We left everything and followed you."

²⁹⁻³¹ Jesus said, "Mark my words, no one who sacrifices house, brothers, sisters, mother, father, children, land—whatever—because of me and the Message will lose out. They'll get it all back, but multiplied many times in homes, brothers, sisters, mothers, children, and land—but also in troubles. And then the bonus of eternal life! This is once again the Great Reversal: Many who are first will end up last, and the last first."

2. What is the most puzzling part of this story to you—seems to contradict what you know about Jesus?

3. Why do you think Jesus gave a list of rules for the man to follow before he narrowed the focus to the man's priorities?

   a. He wanted to get the man's aĀention
   b. He was trying to get a beĀer understanding of the man's personality type.
   c. He wanted to show the man that rule-keeping wasn't as important as giving up his "money-god."
   d. He was affirming the man's good work from the past.
   e. Other _____

4. Do you think Jesus wants everyone to sell everything they have to be his follower? If so, why? If not, what point do you think he's trying to make with the man?

5. It's not hard to understand the disciples' surprise when Jesus told them about pushing a camel through the eye of a needle. But what do you think about Jesus' explanation? What do you think he meant when he said in verse 27: "No chance at all if you think you can pull it off by yourself. Every chance in the world if you let God do it"?

THE ACCOUNTABLE COMMUNITY:

6. When you think about replacing your "money-god" with Jesus' life ("Go sell whatever you own and give it to the poor"), what might be the hardest for you to give up?

Make a list of your top 5 life priorities. Then number them in order from most important (5) to least important (1).

___ a. _____

___ b. _____

___ c. _____

___ d. _____

___ e. _____

Now share your answers with the group.

7. If Jesus sat down with you today, over a cup of coffee, what question out of the Bible reading would you want to ask him?

8. What might be the next step he would ask you to take if you decided to follow him?

   How can this group help you take that step?

   EVERYONE PRAY SILENTLY FOR THE PERSON ON YOUR LEFT.

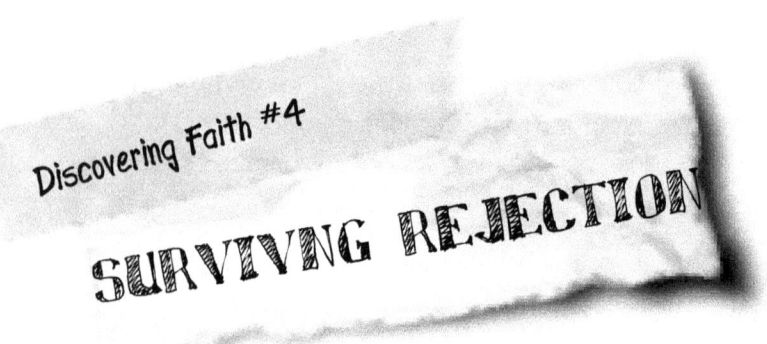

THE BIG IDEA:

We have all faced rejection. Whether it was not being chosen for a playground ball team or losing a relationship, it's always painful. As we take positive steps in discovering faith—in exploring who Jesus is—and who we might be in relation to him, we may face mountains of rejection from those who don't understand. In this study, Jesus went back to the town where he grew up and tried to explain his mission on earth. His hometown crowd just didn't get it—or maybe they just didn't want to get it.

OPEN:

1. When was the first time that you were denied something because of your differences (gender, ethnicity, disability, age, etc.)? What was most painful about it?

READ AND APPLY :: Luke 4:14–30 (MSG)

¹⁴⁻¹⁵ Jesus returned to Galilee powerful in the Spirit. News that he was back spread through the countryside. He taught in their meeting places to everyone's acclaim and pleasure.

¹⁶⁻²¹ He came to Nazareth where he had been reared. As he always did on the Sabbath, he went to the meeting place. When he stood up to read, he was handed the scroll of the prophet Isaiah. Unrolling the scroll, he found the place where it was written,

God's Spirit is on me; he's chosen me
to preach the Message of good news to the poor,
Sent me to announce pardon to prisoners
and recovery of sight to the blind,

> To set the burdened and battered free,
> to announce, "This is God's year to act!"

He rolled up the scroll, handed it back to the assistant, and sat down. Every eye in the place was on him, intent. Then he started in, "You've just heard Scripture make history. It came true just now in this place."

²² All who were there, watching and listening, were surprised at how well he spoke. But they also said, "Isn't this Joseph's son, the one we've known since he was a youngster?"

²³⁻²⁷ He answered, "I suppose you're going to quote the proverb, 'Doctor, go heal yourself. Do here in your hometown what we heard you did in Capernaum.' Well, let me tell you something: No prophet is ever welcomed in his hometown. Isn't it a fact that there were many widows in Israel at the time of Elijah during that three and a half years of drought when famine devastated the land, but the only widow to whom Elijah was sent was in Sarepta in Sidon? And there were many lepers in Israel at the time of the prophet Elisha but the only one cleansed was Naaman the Syrian."

²⁸⁻³⁰ That set everyone in the meeting place seething with anger. They threw him out, banishing him from the village, then took him to a mountain cliff at the edge of the village to throw him to his doom, but he gave them the slip and was on his way.

2. If you had grown up in Nazareth as a friend of Jesus, how would you have felt watching this scene unfold?
   a. Angry! Who is this Jesus pretending to be?
   b. Is this the same kid who climbed trees with me?
   c. Wow, I knew there was something special about Jesus.
   d. I think I would have been just trying to figure out what was happening.
   e. Other _____

3. Using a pencil or pen, take 2 minutes to draw a scribble-picture of your emotions, if you had been Jesus facing his hometown crowd. Hold your picture up so the group can see it; then describe what you drew.

4. Why do you think the crowd was so angry at Jesus?
   a. He was challenging their values.
   b. They liked the social structure the way it was. He was messing it up.
   c. He was just a "punk kid." What right did he have telling them what to do?
   d. I can't understand what the big deal was.
   e. Other _____

5. If you had a chance to determine which people get accepted in YOUR "world," what would you do?
   a. Change society's treatment of people who aren't like me (and do the work that is required).
   b. I'd fit into the upper class and forget about everyone else.

   c. I'd stay who I am; everything in my world is good.
   d. I'd start helping the poor first, like Jesus said.
   e. Other _____

Why did you choose your answer?

THE ACCOUNTABLE COMMUNITY:

6. What are some of the barriers that prevent YOU from stepping into the life of another person or group of people?
   a. I'm an introvert; new people scare me.
   b. I'm not really interested in people who aren't like me.
   c. It might not be safe to connect with others.
   d. I don't know what to say.
   e. Other _____

7. If you decided to identify with Jesus' mission (described in verses 16–21), what/who would probably be the source of your greatest rejection

   What might you need to do to take the next big faith-step?
   a. Be convinced that Jesus is the one I want to follow.
   b. Wait for God to change my attitude
   c. I don't want to take another step right now.
   d. Sit, reflect and pray.
   e. Other _____

8. How can this group help you get past a barrier or take a new step forward in personal faith this week?

   LET EACH PERSON PRAY FOR THE PERSON ON THEIR LEFT. YOU MAY PRAY OUT LOUD OR SILENTLY. IF YOU WANT TO PRAY SILENTLY JUST SAY, "I'M DONE" WHEN YOU'VE PRAYED AND ARE READY FOR THE NEXT PERSON TO TAKE THEIR TURN. THE GROUP LEADER WILL END THE PRAYER TIME.

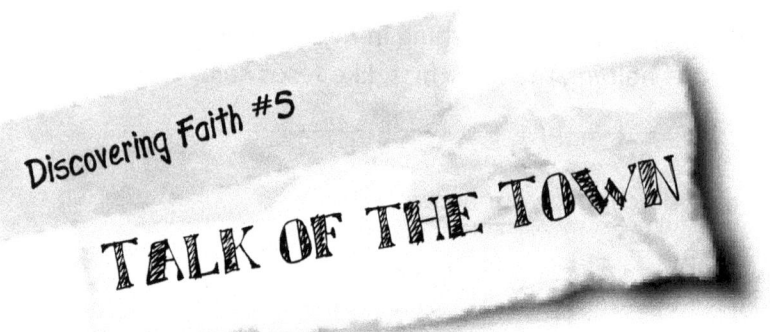

Discovering Faith #5

TALK OF THE TOWN

THE BIG IDEA:
We rarely run into people who are raving mad. They are put into a hospital or prison. In this story, the town's people didn't know how to deal with a man who was controlled by many evil spirits. They tried chaining him up in the cemetery, but each time he broke loose. So he was always part of the town gossip; wondering if they were safe from him. Notice how the "talk of the town" changes by story's end.

OPEN:

1. Before you turned 12, what was the most significant event in your life? Why was it so important?

READ AND APPLY :: Mark 5:1-20 (MSG)

¹⁻⁵They arrived on the other side of the sea in the country of the Gerasenes. As Jesus got out of the boat, a madman from the cemetery came up to him. He lived there among the tombs and graves. No one could restrain him—he couldn't be chained, couldn't be tied down. He had been tied up many times with chains and ropes, but he broke the chains, snapped the ropes. No one was strong enough to tame him. Night and day he roamed through the graves and the hills, screaming out and slashing himself with sharp stones.
⁶⁻⁸When he saw Jesus a long way off, he ran and bowed in worship before him—then bellowed in protest, "What business do you have, Jesus, Son of the High God, messing with me? I swear to God, don't

give me a hard time!" (Jesus had just commanded the tormenting evil spirit, "Out! Get out of the man!")

⁹⁻¹⁰Jesus asked him, "Tell me your name."

He replied, "My name is Mob. I'm a rioting mob." Then he desperately begged Jesus not to banish them from the country.

¹¹⁻¹³A large herd of pigs was browsing and rooting on a nearby hill. The demons begged him, "Send us to the pigs so we can live in them." Jesus gave the order. But it was even worse for the pigs than for the man. Crazed, they stampeded over a cliff into the sea and drowned.

¹⁴⁻¹⁵Those tending the pigs, scared to death, bolted and told their story in town and country. Everyone wanted to see what had happened. They came up to Jesus and saw the madman sitting there wearing decent clothes and making sense, no longer a walking madhouse of a man.

¹⁶⁻¹⁷Those who had seen it told the others what had happened to the demon-possessed man and the pigs. At first they were in awe—and then they were upset, upset over the drowned pigs. They demanded that Jesus leave and not come back.

¹⁸⁻²⁰As Jesus was getting into the boat, the demon-delivered man begged to go along, but he wouldn't let him. Jesus said, "Go home to your own people. Tell them your story—what the Master did, how he had mercy on you." The man went back and began to preach in the Ten Towns area about what Jesus had done for him. He was the talk of the town.

2. If Jesus hadn't come along, what do you think would have happened to this man? How would the town's people finally have controlled him?

3. What part of this story most captures your imagination
   a. The mad man running through the tombs.
   b. Jesus' bold encounter with the evil spirits.
   c. The pigs jumping into the sea.
   d. The pig farmers who lost their livelihood.
   e. The people who wanted Jesus to leave.
   f. Other _____

4. Why do you think Jesus was willing to follow the request of the evil spirits to be sent into the pigs, rather than banishing them somewhere else?

   Why might he have been willing to sacrifice the pigs?
   a. Jesus was a Jew who didn't eat pork, so the pigs were no big deal.
   b. Jesus wanted to prove that he had power over evil spirits.
   c. Jesus' priority was to bring the man back to health.
   d. I don't know the point; it doesn't make sense.
   e. Other _____

5. If you were this freed madman and were writing a FOUR LINE poem to express how your life was changed, what would you write?

   _____

   _____

   _____

   _____

THE ACCOUNTABLE COMMUNITY:

6. Of the various people in this story, whom do you most identi y with?
   - the town's people
   - the madman
   - the freed "madman"
   - the pig farmers
   - the on-lookers
   - Jesus' followers

Why do you identi y with them? What part of this story most resembles your current life situation

7. If Jesus drew up to your house today, and said, "Hey, I'm here to set you free," what would you first want him to free you from?

   What doubts might still remain that he could really do it?

8. How can this group best pray for you and help you believe that Jesus could bring you freedom?

   What do you need them to do to support you this week?

   IN CLOSING, LET 2 OR 3 VOLUNTEERS PRAY FOR
   THE GROUP MEMBERS.

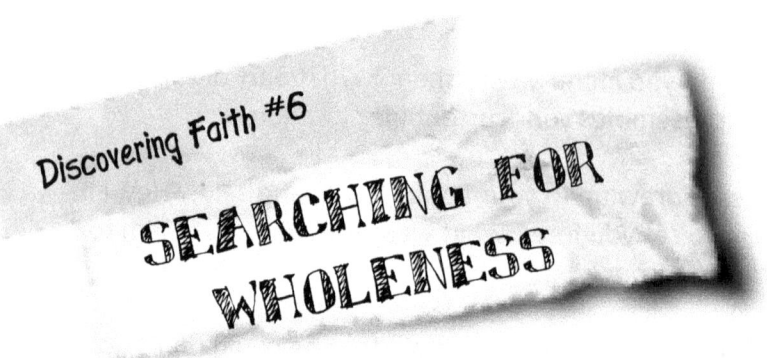

Discovering Faith #6

SEARCHING FOR WHOLENESS

THE BIG IDEA:
We return to a story of Jesus' encounter with a woman. This time, not only is she a woman (considered of little value in Jewish culture), she is sick with a bleeding disorder—probably some sort of vaginal hemorrhaging. Her illness makes her "unclean" so she can no longer aĀend worship at the Jewish synagogue (church) or live a "normal" life. We find her sneaking into the crowd and touching Jesus (a man) in a last-ditch aĀempt to find wholeness.

OPEN:

1. What is the worst injury or illness that you've had? If you've recovered, who was your biggest help toward your recovery?

READ AND APPLY :: Luke 8:43-48 (MSG)

⁴³⁻⁴⁵ In the crowd that day there was a woman who for twelve years had been afflicted with hemorrhages. She had spent every penny she had on doctors but not one had been able to help her. She slipped in from behind and touched the edge of Jesus' robe. At that very moment her hemorrhaging stopped. Jesus said, "Who touched me?"

When no one stepped forward, Peter said, "But Master, we've got crowds of people on our hands. Dozens have touched you."

⁴⁶ Jesus insisted, "Someone touched me. I felt power discharging from me."

⁴⁷ When the woman realized that she couldn't remain hidden, she knelt trembling before him. In front of all the people, she blurted out her story—why she touched him and how at that same moment she was healed.

⁴⁸ *Jesus said, "Daughter, you took a risk trusting me, and now you're healed and whole. Live well, live blessed!"*

2. If you were a **MAN** in the crowd around Jesus, how do you think you would have responded to the "unclean" woman sneaking up to touch Jesus?

   If you were a **WOMAN**, do you think you would have responded differently?

3. Try to put yourself into this woman's sandals. What 3 or 4 big concerns would have been racing through your mind as you approached Jesus from behind?

   a.

   b.

   c.

   d.

4. Jesus said that the women took a risk in trusting him. What do you think was risky?
   a. Whether she would later be accepted at local coāee stands.
   b. The crowds' view of her touching a man without permission.
   c. Opening her heart to Jesus.
   d. That she might not be healed (the eāort was worthless).
   e. Other _____

5. Why do you think Jesus made a "scene" about this woman touching him? (He could have just kept quiet.)

6. When you look at Jesus' dialog with the woman, what other healing, besides physical, do you think she may have experienced?

THE ACCOUNTABLE COMMUNITY:

7. As you consider a struggle that you're experiencing, what part of this story encourages you to think that there might be WHOLENESS available for you?

8. How does Jesus' statement to "live well, live blessed," speak into your need for wholeness? What specific healing might be most important for you right now?
    - healing of emotional pain
    - healing of physical issues
    - the ability to overcome temptatio
    - believing that there is a God who cares
    - healing from old ways of thinking
    - healing of depressed feelings
    - I don't know of anything right now
    - other _____

9. From this time together with your group, how can they help you experience the healing or wholeness that you need?

    How can they encourage you through this week?

    LET 2 OR 3 VOLUNTEERS PRAY FOR SPECIFIC NEEDS IN THE GROUP. THE LEADER WILL CLOSE.

Discovering Faith #7
HEALING THOSE STRAINED RELATIONSHIPS

THE BIG IDEA:
Human relationshi s often have the greatest impact on whether we discover faith or not. For example, it's hard to believe that there is a God "out there" who cares about us, if we don't have parents who cared unconditionally for us. Or we may struggle to keep healthy relationshi s with siblings, would-be life partners, spouses, or kids. All influence how we feel about creating a relationship with a God we cannot see, who supposedly loves us and wants the very best for us.

In this story, Jacob is a thief and a cheat. He stole his twin brother's (Esau) inheritance and blessing (a big deal in Jewish culture). Then, because his momma liked him best, she protected him from being killed by Esau and sent him to live with his uncle for many years. The story picks up as Jacob (with his wives and family) returns to his homeland and sees his twin brother off in the distance, coming to meet him.

OPEN:

1. Think back to a time when you were facing a dreaded family gathering. What turned out to be the best part? What was the worst part?

READ AND APPLY :: Genesis 33:1-17 (MSG)
$^{1-4}$ Jacob looked up and saw Esau coming with his four hundred men. He divided the children between Leah and Rachel and the

two maidservants. He put the maidservants out in front, Leah and her children next, and Rachel and Joseph last. He led the way and, as he approached his brother, bowed seven times, honoring his brother. But Esau ran up and embraced him, held him tight and kissed him. And they both wept

⁵ Then Esau looked around and saw the women and children: "And who are these with you?"

Jacob said, "The children that God saw fit to bless me with."

⁶⁻⁷ Then the maidservants came up with their children and bowed; then Leah and her children, also bowing; and finally, Joseph and Rachel came up and bowed to Esau.

⁸ Esau then asked, "And what was the meaning of all those herds that I met?"

"I was hoping that they would pave the way for my master to welcome me."

⁹ Esau said, "Oh, brother. I have plenty of everything—keep what is yours for yourself."

¹⁰⁻¹¹ Jacob said, "Please. If you can find it in your heart to welcome me, accept these gifts. When I saw your face, it was as the face of God smiling on me. Accept the gifts I have brought for you. God has been good to me and I have more than enough." Jacob urged the gifts on him and Esau accepted.

¹² Then Esau said, "Let's start out on our way; I'll take the lead."

¹³⁻¹⁴ But Jacob said, "My master can see that the children are frail. And the flocks and herds are nursing, making for slow going. If I push them too hard, even for a day, I'd lose them all. So, master, you go on ahead of your servant, while I take it easy at the pace of my flocks and children. I'll catch up with you in Seir."

¹⁵ Esau said, "Let me at least lend you some of my men."

"There's no need," said Jacob. "Your generous welcome is all I need or want."

¹⁶ So Esau set out that day and made his way back to Seir.

¹⁷ And Jacob left for Succoth. He built a shelter for himself and sheds for his livestock. That's how the place came to be called Succoth (Sheds).

2. What do you think were the first words out of Jacob's mouth when he came up over the hill and saw Esau with 400 men coming toward his family and flocks?
   a. "Oh good, he's in time for the picnic."
   b. "You wives and kids stay out in front of me, just in case this thing goes bad."
   c. "Oh #%$#@%!"
   d. "I Hope God has a plan in mind for the next 5 minutes."
   e. Other _____

3. Although Jacob is a changed person in many ways, what do you see that still shows evidence of his conniving attitud

4. Jacob is "blown away" by Esau's attitude; he doesn't seem to believe what Esau says. Why do you think Esau was so changed from when Jacob ran away years before?
   a. "Time heals all wounds."
   b. Both men had grown up over the years.
   c. It was no challenge for him to wipe out the women, children and Jacob.
   d. God had given Esau a new perspecti e.
   e. Other _____

5. If you were doing a picture collage of this "family gathering" (between Jacob and Esau) what 5 pictures would you save for the family album? Describe them.

   a.

   b.

   c.

   d.

   e.

ACCOUNTABLE COMMUNITY:

6. What comes to your mind as you think about the next holiday with the extended family?
    a. It's gonna be so good.
    b. I wish I didn't have to go!
    c. I can hardly wait for the home cookin'.
    d. It's time we got some things resolved.
    e. Other _____

7. What seems to hold you back from mending strained relationships?
    a. I'm ready, but they're not.
    b. It's too late.
    c. The timing just isn't right.
    d. It's too painful.
    e. Other _____

8. What results would you need to see, to believe that God could do a miracle in a strained or broken relationships?

    How can the group help YOU take the first step toward trusting God to begin the mending?

LET VOLUNTEERS PRAY FOR SPECIFIC NEEDS IN THE GROUP. ONE MEMBER CLOSES THE SESSION AFTER VOLUNTEERS HAVE PRAYED.

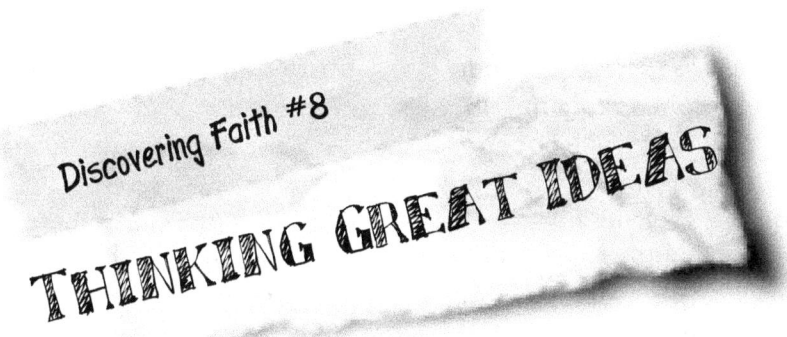

Discovering Faith #8
THINKING GREAT IDEAS

THE BIG IDEA:
The Bible is clear that God wants to make us different, but we must also put eāort into our spiritual well-being. And one way we can put ourselves in the best place for God's creati e work is by focusing our minds on great things—by looking for God's big dreams that are planted in us.

One of Jesus' followers, St. Paul (who wrote several leāers in the New Testament section of the Bible), gives us a clear perspecti e on how to focus our thoughts for the most spiritual impact.

OPEN:

1. Answer ONE of the following two questions
   - Outside of the Bible, what book has had the most profound impact upon how you live? Why? OR
   - What person, dead or alive, do you see as the most important mentor for you? Why?

READ AND APPLY :: Philippians 4:4-9 (MSG)

4-5 Celebrate God all day, every day. I mean, revel in him! Make it as clear as you can to all you meet that you're on their side, working with them and not against them. Help them see that the Master is about to arrive. He could show up any minute!
6-7 Don't fret or worry. Instead of worrying, pray. Let petitions and praises shape your worries into prayers, letting God know

your concerns. Before you know it, a sense of God's wholeness, everything coming together for good, will come and settle you down. It's wonderful what happens when Christ displaces worry at the center of your life.

8-9 Summing it all up, friends, I'd say you'll do best by filling your minds and meditating on things true, noble, reputable, authentic, compelling, gracious—the best, not the worst; the beautiful, not the ugly; things to praise, not things to curse. Put into practice what you learned from me, what you heard and saw and realized. Do that, and God, who makes everything work together, will work you into his most excellent harmonies.

2. If these words arrived today in a leAer from your best friend, what would be your reaction
   a. "Thanks for your positive perspecti e!"
   b. "Well, thanks—but, I need a solution right now!"
   c. "Wow, I will pray that God helps me see it this way!"
   d. "Sounds like coAon-candy; just so much fluff."
   e. "Buzz off; you have no idea what I'm going through!"
   f. Other _____

3. What might Paul mean when he says that practicing these things "works us into God's most excellent harmonies"?
   a. Our lives are like songs—we create good or bad notes.
   b. We begin to align with God's dreams for us.
   c. Somehow, God orchestrates a symphony out of my mess!
   d. Other _____

4. When you get caught in a negati e-thinking trap, what helps you get your mind out of it?

   On the next page, list 3 or 4 tools that help you.

1.

2.

3.

4.

THE ACCOUNTABLE COMMUNITY:

5. Scan through the passage again quickly. What words point to an area of your life that needs improvement?

   What difference would you expect to see if you followed the directions that Paul gives?

6. How might changing your thinking make it easier to discover a faith-foundation in Jesus?

7. What is the next right step that you would like to make in Discovering Your Faith?

8. How can this group help you take that next right step, and hold you accountable to keep moving forward in your faith journey?

   Let the leader start the prayer time with THANKSGIVING TO GOD for the group's time together and the good things that are happening in the group members.

Then, if the group members feel comfortable, each can pray out loud like this for the person on their right:

"Dear God, this is _____.

Please help _____ so he/she grows to be more and more like Jesus. Thanks!"

> GROUP LEADER:
> Make sure that the group takes time to celebrate the weeks that they have been together. The following CELEBRATION NOTES may help.

CELEBRATE THE GROUP

Now that you've been together as a group for at least eight weeks, it's time to celebrate the group.

If you don't already have some food, you need to get some—and beverages.

Then, take some time to reflect back on what you're Discovering about Faith.

Discuss some questions like the following:

- Where have you seen changes in your thoughts about faith?

- Does thinking about trusting Jesus with your life seem safer now, or more frightening?

- What more do you wish you could know about a life that follows Jesus?

- What was the most helpful thing the group did for you during this time together?

- What are the top 3 BIG TIME memories you'll take with you?

    _____

    _____

    _____

- What life areas do you want to keep working on—to keep growing in?

- How might this group help you, to keep you taking the right steps forward?

- What should this group be doing for the future?

    Continue to meet around a new topic.
    Finish this celebration and stop meeting; we'll continue to be good friends.
    Look for friends to join the group.
    Take a break, then get back together in _____.
    Other _____

GROUP LEADER NOTES
TO GET YOU STARTED

FIRST!
It makes no difference if you're guiding an administrati e board, a sports-bar Bible study, or something in between. Every group needs to function as a community of people who live in love with one another. So the following guidelines are adaptable to any setting

WHAT IT'S NOT
These study sessions are NOT a place for you to teach the Bible to a group of people. The PRIMARY PURPOSE of these sessions is to create healthy relationshi s (with God and other humans) around scripture—to connect the "3 stories" (see "A Little Group Theory" below). People will learn the Bible as it makes real connection to their lives.

AS THE LEADER
(the one who is responsible for getting the group together)
Your job is not to lecture, give advice, or anything else that sounds like teaching. You're the facilitator of this group of people.

HANG ONTO YOUR CHAIR
The idea of creating a small group may be a whole new (and scary) thought for you—especially a group outside the walls of your congregation. You may have been pushed into this role by someone who gives you a paycheck. Someone may have challenged you to a stretching experiment. Or you may have been wondering how to get your ministry to a deeper level. If any of those scenarios are true, just hang on and watch what can happen in the next few weeks.

GUIDE THE GROUP

As the team leader, you will guide the group session (topic, time usage, etc.). Keep the group on track and within the time limits, even if each question is not answered or each activity completed. It is important to give time signals (at least 5 minutes and 2 minutes) when you must cut off discussion. Every session must START and STOP on time. If some want to continue with discussion after the scheduled conclusion time, dismiss everyone and let those who want to stay, stay. This allows the group to respect those who must leave.

People will be energized for the next group session if they haven't felt trapped or been frustrated that they were just "killing time." Of course, you may hear some groans when time is cut short. Explain what you're doing—keeping your word to end the session on time. The complaining means that discussion was going well.

PLEASE ...

- Make sure that each person has a book or printout of the week's session. Everyone should have the same scripture version. IN FACT, ask people NOT to bring other biblical commentaries, books, etc., to the group, so everyone can stay focused on the specific Bible passage and questions. Commentaries tend to shut down conversation because people believe they have the "correct answer" to questions

If you're an old pro at this small group study, we trust that the materials in this book will be a resource to help you move your group into a joyful and transparent community—to become a group of people who care deeply for one another and serve from that community— both to one another and to others outside the group.

- Respect each person for what they say, no matter how "off-base" it may seem.

- Set the time and place for the next group meeting

- Care for group members and their families between meetings. That doesn't mean you do it all yourself. You encourage and coordinate (or have someone coordinate) the group members in their care of one another.

- Go FIRST in answering questions early on. It helps break the ice when you give an example of how you would answer a question

- Break the group into 4s or 5s (try to never use 3s) for Bible study and the related questions. Then everyone will have a chance to contribute. Even the introverts who are nervous about speaking publicly will usually join in. Using 3s puts people into intimidating triangles.

- Carefully note "The Accountable Community" section near the end of each session. This is extremely important for the group's life and ministry. Details are given below.

A LITTLE GROUP THEORY

A. CONNECTING the THREE STORIES THROUGH GUIDED QUESTIONS

There are three stories that MUST connect if people are to discover what it means to be a whole person, and live in a vital, growing community.

THE QUESTIONS are intentionally worded and placed where they are to help the THREE STORIES CONNECT around the Bible.

- The FIRST story is God's story (told through the Bible) that shows God's plan to create us as amazing humans, describes our walking away from God's plan, and explains God's becoming human to call us back home to wholeness.

- The second story is another person's life story, with all its stuff.

- The third story is "my" story, with all of "my" stuff.

When the three stories come together, amazing transformation happens.

- This model of small group is built on the fact that we need to tell our story, and connect that story to other people and to God.

- All of us have a child inside who wants to be released. These studies will help us "come to Jesus as a little child." So prepare to laugh and cry!

- CAUTIONS:
    1. We do NOT let people confess another person's "sins."
    2. People are only allowed to talk about their own issues.
    3. Gossip can kill a group. Often prayer requests are actually cloaked gossip. We must not allow people to talk about other people.
    4. Sometimes a person may dominate conversation with their own struggles—in a specific meeting or meeting after meeting. As a leader, you may need to talk directly to such a person, in private. A group cannot do therapy for an individual. That takes special care from a professional.

- As we tell our stories in the biblical context, the scriptures will become real to us. The goal of these studies is NOT to teach the Bible as a cognitive activity, just filling peoples' heads with memorized content.

- While some of the questions would seem needless if we're just trying to teach Bible, **they are important for building relationships**. And there is a specific sequence to the questions

OPEN:
The **Open** question(s) is to get the group thinking about the biblical topic in a non-threatening way; often producing laughter, bringing out positive endorphins and reducing barriers to the deeper questions that are coming.

READ & APPLY:
The **Feeling** questions (those first 2 or 3 right aÃer the Bible reading) are very important in helping people put themselves into the scripture passage.

The next **Scripture Content** questions are just that—questions to dig out some of the content. You may want to add more here, but do it carefully so you don't bog down the small group or lose sight of the overall purpose. The temptation is to "go deeper" in study, which usually means learning facts instead of allowing the Bible to transform our lives."

Many questions are given, but you are the leader and you should know your group. Since you KNOW THE PURPOSE (above) of the various questions, feel free to rewrite or adapt the questions for your needs. HOWEVER, as you adapt, keep the flow of questions going in the right order. You'll be glad you did.

THE ACCOUNTABLE COMMUNITY:
- **Personal Application** questions are where the scripture gets personal.

- **Community Accountability** pulls everything together with the group committing themselves to stand together for each person's personal growth and the group's health.

- During this time, you have the opportunity to guide the group in caring for one another.

B. READING THE BIBLE...

It's not unusual for people to be called on to read in a group. However, it can strike terror in any introvert or person with reading difficulties. Use these guidelines when preparing to read the Bible passages together as a group.

1. Unless you know a person really well, and their reading ability, never call on a person to read "cold turkey." This is especially true when reading the Bible, which may have difficu -to-pronounce words or complicated language structures.

2. The best way to prepare a person to read is pre-heating them before the session starts. Give them the opportunity to review the passage and plan for any difficult words or phrases.

3. If a person volunteers to read but then has difficulty getting through a passage, feel free to assist them by giving them a word or two and letting them aĀempt to continue

4. Thank and compliment readers, particularly when the passage or pronunciations have been difficult.

C. A WORD ABOUT PRAYING TOGETHER

From session to session you will want to change the way the group PRAYS. Sometimes you'll want the group all together. Other weeks staying in the 4s will be best.

If you want to make your group members "go spitless" just ask them to pray out loud. But if you want to teach them to actually pray for one another, suggest various forms of prayer in a progressive way.

Level 1:
   After the group has shared concerns, close by praying yourself.

Level 2:
   Ask for specific requests then ask for specific volunteers to pray for those requests.

Level 3:
   Ask two or three group members to pray, then you conclude. Don't be afraid of silence for a moment or two.

Level 4:
   Ask the group to sit or stand in a circle and pray out loud around the circle by saying something like, "Dear God, this is _____. Thank you for _____. Amen."
   If anyone is uncomfortable with this plan, they can just say "Pass" when their turn comes.

You can also try variations of any of these, such as having the group pray silently around the circle for the person on their left.

Before long you'll have the whole group easily praying for one another. They just have to discover that it's safe to say what they're really thinking and feeling without the pressure to produce some form of "magic" words for God.

D. THE MISSION

Mission is vital to Christian growth. As a goal, each person should be serving someone else each week. In addition, the entire group should be serving together at least once each month. Of course, your group may not reach this goal right away.

Think about possible ways you can serve your neighborhood, city, and world together. There are some suggestions in the "We Serve Together" section (p. 48.)

The basic mission of the group comes in the form of an empty chair at each session. Each group member should constantly be on the lookout for friends and neighbors to fill the empty chair—to join your community of care.

It is important to plant the idea of MISSION or SERVICE at the very fi st gathering of the group. And continue to remind people of it each time the group meets.

E. BIRTHING NEW GROUPS

Much can be said about birthing new groups, but here are a few important guidelines.

Never use the term "split a group." Birthing is the healthy beginning of another group, out of an original group.

Once groups reach 10 to 12 people, the group needs to start planning the birth. However, "birthing" should be discussed at the very fi st group meetin , and every meeting thereaAer, so no one is surprised.

Every group must have a group "Apprentice" as well as a "Leader." When birthing a new group, the original leader, with three to six people from the original group, leave to start the new group. The apprentice stays to lead the original group. Both groups must then quickly find new apprentice leaders.

Birthing is easier if the original group and the newly-birthed group create a celebration party for the launch. You also might consider periodic "family reunion" parties for a couple of months.

Everyone is responsible for recruiting new group members to fill the vacancies created by the birth—and to grow the new-birthed group. Never forget the empty chair.

F. LAST BUT NOT LEAST

To be most effective in your ministry as a group leader, start seeing yourself as a pastor to your group. That's right, we said PASTOR.

Try saying that out loud to yourself:
"I am a pastor to this small group of people."

Congratulations, you did it!

You're not just a leader of meetings or the coordinator of some production, your first role should be caring for the needs (particularly the Christian formation) of your group/team.

But before you reject the idea outright, think about it for a minute. Your congregation probably has another person whom you call pastor. She or he oversees the larger ministry of the congregation. However, there is no way that one person can meet all of a congregation s many needs. The best care comes when a small group, led by its leader, takes responsibility for its team members. You are the "front-line pastor" to your "congregation."

This pastoring model may take the shape primarily of leading the small group sessions. But it should also include staying alert to the individual emotional, spiritual, etc., needs of your team members. In addition, it may mean hospital visitation or rallying the group for special support of a team member who is facing a crisis.

Here's another way to think of it: You are a COACH!

When you read that word COACH, your mind may race to individuals you've seen pace the sidelines of a court or field; some yelling, screaming and throwing things—others calmly watching and guiding the team.

But hundreds of years before the word COACH became a person, it was a vehicle. And that vehicle carried royalty—PRECIOUS CARGO.

Let that idea soak in your brain for a while.

Do we need to say it? When you are pastoring/coaching your group, you are carrying precious "cargo." You are helping God's Spirit move people from where they are right now to where God wants them to be, down the road.

But don't let that overwhelm you. This is God's ministry and we have the privilege of partnering with the Holy Spirit—who was at work long before we got to this place—and a team of people who can learn to care for one another.

So model care and guide your group. Have fun watching what you and God can do together, to grow your group into a wonderfully caring community!

WE SERVE TOGETHER

Between group meetings, each group member is working to serve someplace in their community. IN ADDITION, the group should be dreaming of ways they can serve together, at least once while they are together in this study.

You probably, already know a great service agency in your area. If not, check out this short list of ideas to get you started.

One or two group members will need to take the assignment to research and contact the agreed-upon agency or agencies—to arrange the best time for working. Then others can jump in to care for the details of travel to and from the site, covering meals, childcare, needed equipment, etc.

Let this time of service be a great event, and maybe the beginning of something more long-term.

Have a great time!!!

- **Most any community has an agency that serves homeless people.** You will need to research the options and the requirements for volunteers to serve. Look first for an agency that does more than serve meals, but that cares for the whole person. Certainly serving meals is important to those who are hungry, so don't discount those groups either.

- **Give Kids the World.** If you're not from Florida, this could be a group "workcation." Or you could help a family take their special needs child to GKW.

"The Village" is a 70-acre resort complete with over 140 Villa accommodations, entertainment att actions, whimsical venues, and fun specifically designed for children with special needs. Located in Kissimmee, FL, Give Kids The World has welcomed more than 100,000 families from all 50 states and over 70 countries.

Give Kids The World can offer the perfect volunteering experience for church, civic, youth and many other types of groups. They provide a fulfilling and rewarding event for your group while accomplishing needed tasks and projects at their facility.
http://www.gktw.org

• **Look for an opportunity to work with the aging or homebound.** Many communities have agencies that you can partner with to serve this growing population group.

• **KaBOOM!** Do you know of a run-down playground or a place that really needs one? KaBOOM helps communities build playgrounds. They have contests to determine which communities receive the playgrounds and then look for volunteers to help build them. **http://kaboom.org**

• **Feeding America (formerly Second Harvest).** There are opportunities to help distribute food to those in need. Check out their website for the location nearest you.
http://feedingamerica.org

• **Habitat for Humanity.** You can help make a huge difference in a family's life by helping to build them a home. Habitat has a long history of great service and use of volunteers. Check out the website for the location nearest you. **http://habitat.org**

www.ingramcontent.com/pod-product-compliance
Lightning Source LLC
Chambersburg PA
CBHW061515040426
42450CB00008B/1638